TON

BY BRIAN JOHNSTON

Copyright © 2017 HAYES PRESS

All rights reserved. No part of this book may be reproduced, stored in a retrieval system, or transmitted in any form, without the written permission of Search for Truth UK.

Published by:

HAYES PRESS CHRISTIAN PUBLISHERS

The Barn, Flaxlands

Royal Wootton Bassett

Swindon, SN4 8DY

United Kingdom

www.hayespress.org

Scriptures marked NIV are from New International Version®, NIV® Copyright © 1973, 1978, 1984, 2011 by Biblica, Inc.™ Used by permission. All rights reserved worldwide. Scriptures marked NASB are from the New American Standard Bible®, Copyright © 1960, 1962, 1963, 1968, 1971, 1972, 1973, 1975, 1977, 1995 by The Lockman Foundation. Used by permission (www.Lockman.org).

PREFACE

It is wise not to be overly dogmatic in terms of second-guessing the details of God's prophetic outline. As some have rightly said, there is scope for two views in some matters. In this book Brian has majored on what will be seen as the traditional understanding of the so-called 'Pre-millennialist position,' one which envisages Europe playing a key role.

In 'Daniel Decoded' his later book on related topics, Brian has developed more largely the alternative view which envisages an Islamic Caliphate emerging as the focal point of opposition towards Israel. Both views should be understood, and assessed against the Bible texts.

CHAPTER ONE: PRESENCE, REVELATION AND MANIFESTATION

In this book we hope to look at Bible prophecies and their relationship with the broad outline of world trends - not only as they are emerging today, but also as they have been developing over the last 15, 50 or 100 years and more. Perhaps your first reaction to that is to ask: "Is it so important? Isn't it more important to learn how to live our lives today?" I appreciate that concern. But someone has calculated that more than 25% of the Bible, when written, was about predicting events. Even so, God was aiming more at changing hearts than satisfying any curiosity about the future; with the intention, I'm sure, of preparing those hearts to worship him. The realization that God controls the future should bow our hearts in worship. That's what it did for the apostle Paul. In Romans chapter 11 he had been considering God's future purposes for Jew and non-Jew, and when he gets to verse 33 he bursts out into praise: *"Oh the depth of the riches both of the wisdom and knowledge of God!"*

That verse is well-known, but I want to remind you of what leads up to it: Paul was rehearsing prophetically God's plan for the salvation of both Jews and Gentiles. In addition to worship, Bible prophecy is also meant to inspire hope and encouragement. Take another of Paul's letters – one which shows how he used teaching on prophecy to stimulate hope and encouragement among his readers. Paul had a lot to say about future events when writing to his friends in Thessalonica, but it's absolutely clear this was no irrelevant or academic discussion. Very real fears were dispelled by this fuller instruction on the outline of future events as they have been arranged by Almighty God.

What an encouragement it would have been for those disciples to be assured, for example, that their believing friends who had already died were not in any way going to miss out at Christ's return (1 Thessalonians 4:15). At the close of every chapter of his first letter to them, Paul drew their attention to the coming again of Jesus Christ - and he did so for the sake of sharing hope and encouragement. That's quite a remarkable feature of First Thessalonians: every chapter ends by focusing on our Lord's return. The apostle's application of prophecy was designed to quicken their spiritual pulse, and set their sights beyond the here and now. There's a real sense in which the more we live for the world to come, the better we'll live in this present world. Those early Christians at Thessalonica, and elsewhere, had an advantage over us in that they were much closer than we are to the language in which the Bible was originally written. In that original Bible language three different words spell out what's going to happen at the Lord's return. And these words are: presence ('parousia'), revelation ('apokalupsis') and manifestation ('epiphaneia'). The first of these words emphasizes not so much the simple fact of the Lord's return but especially his presence with all the Christian believers of this age - although, obviously, he must return first for this actual presence to become a reality. Listen to the description of this return for believers which the Bible gives us in 1 Thessalonians chapter 4:15-17:

> *"... we who are alive and remain until the coming* [from 'parousia' - the start of the period] *of the Lord will by no means precede those who are asleep. For the Lord Himself will descend from heaven with a shout, with the voice of an archangel, and with the trumpet of God. And the dead in Christ will rise first. Then we who are alive and remain shall be caught up together with them in the clouds to meet the Lord in the air. And thus we shall always be with the Lord."*

'Parousia' is often simply translated as 'coming', but it more fully signifies 'presence' in contradistinction to 'absence' (precisely as in Philippians 2:12). The experience of this presence - this being 'with the Lord' - begins at the time we have been reading about, which many people refer to as 'the Rapture': which means the 'snatching up of Christ's Church' by Christ Himself. 'Snatching up' is in fact a good way to describe what will happen because all believers at the Lord's coming will be caught up in the clouds to meet the Lord in the air. He does not at that time come all the way down to the earth. He comes to the air and calls all believers on himself to him. It's then that we, the believers, enter into this specific period of being in his presence. The Bible talks about things which will take place 'during His presence with His saints' - which is the best way of translating the end of 1 Thessalonians 3:13 (with the emphasis here being on the duration of the period). This special time of his presence with us after the Rapture-event will, of course, be hidden from the eyes of the world. Life on this planet will go on after all true Christians have been taken away from it. The salt of the earth will have gone, and the earth will become more and more corrupt. At least seven years

TOMORROW'S HEADLINES: THE FUTURE IN BIBLE PROPHECY

will run their course on earth, for the Bible describes them in detail, as we'll consider later. Terrible judgements and world-wide catastrophes will rock the globe, and the world, or a great many in it, will find themselves looking to a world leader for deliverance; a leader who is quite definitely in opposition to God and His Christ. When his true colours are revealed it will cost many their lives in trying to escape. During all this time, as the earth ripens for God's judgement, the hidden presence of Christ with believers from the Church Age will continue. But then, at a particular moment signalled in advance by God, his presence with us is going to be revealed to the world. It will be dramatically signalled and unveiled before a watching world.

"For as the lightning comes from the east and flashes to the west, so also will the coming [parousia - here the close of the period is being referred to] *of the Son of Man be"* (Matthew 24:27). The second key Bible word is this word revelation, as we'll see. A time will come when the Lord, after having come for us, will unveil to the rest of the world his presence with us. As a result of this revelation the glory of the Lord is going to be manifested: it's going to become visible. Those are the three Bible words mentioned earlier: presence, revelation and manifestation. As they apply in our Bibles to the Lord's return, we have first of all this special time of his presence with us in the period after the Rapture when he catches us up to be with Himself, hidden from the world. Then comes the moment of revelation to the world as described in Revelation 1:6,7: *"He is coming with clouds, and every eye will see Him, even they who pierced Him. And all the tribes of the earth will mourn because of Him."*

There's no mention of any other than the Lord and the believer in connection with his presence with the Church after he comes and takes it to be with himself. Removed and hidden from the world, we will enjoy his presence with us until the moment when the covering veil is drawn aside (the revealing of Romans 8:19; 2 Thessalonians 1:7) and the Lord Jesus is revealed to the world in flaming fire from heaven. The effect of this revelation will be that the presence of Christ which we've been enjoying will become visible - or manifest - to the whole world, for the Bible talks of *"the brightness of His coming"* (2 Thessalonians 2:8). It's at that time the words of Colossians 3:4 find their fulfilment: *"When Christ who is our life appears* [or is made manifest], *then you also will appear with Him in glory."*

To see it in the orderly two-stage way the Bible presents it, we need to distinguish between those words presence, revelation and manifestation. The manifestation of the glory of the Lord is the result of the revelation, and what is being revealed or unveiled is his presence which has been with us ever since the event known as 'the Rapture of the Church' (See the appendix to this chapter). I hope these thoughts about this first prophetic event for which we, as believers, are waiting, will fill us with a sense of assurance; for they were designed to do just that for the first century believers at Thessalonica and elsewhere. As well as inspiring our worship, a consideration of Bible prophecy is clearly meant to stimulate such a sense of hope and encouragement in us. And there are even more good biblical reasons to look into the prophetic sections of the Bible. For example, the apostle Peter was even more explicit in saying how knowledge of the future is meant to shape our lives now. When he spoke of the world to come, he stressed it was so that his readers might know what sort of people they ought to be in holy conduct and godliness (2 Peter 3:11).

In fact, earlier, in his first letter, Peter had already spoken of interest among angels at looking into the fulfilment of the message of the Old Testament prophets (1 Peter 1:10-12). Now, if that's the case, it can hardly be inappropriate for us to spend some time considering the prophetic sections of the Bible. The interest and desire Peter records the angels having was a Christ-centred one. And that's the very best reason for our interest in prophecy too. The more we study it, the more we find it's centred on Christ. That's the inescapable conclusion we have to draw from the apostle John's visions of the future in the Bible's last book. It's called 'Revelation' as we know, and that's because it's a revelation of Jesus Christ. He's gloriously revealed as being central to God's plan of the ages! The testimony of Jesus is the spirit of prophecy (Revelation 19:10). Nothing reveals his majesty better than when we come to see the prominent place that belongs to him in God's eternal purposes. The Bible tells us that the secret things belong to God, but those things which he's revealed belong to us. Surely, then, it's right to make our own those matters God's revealed about his future dealings with this world.

APPENDIX TO CHAPTER 1
A 2-phase Second Advent:

- is consistent with a literal & dispensational interpretation
- distinguishes God's plans for Israel & the Church
- explains the absence of any mention of 'Church' in Revelation 6-18
- allows for the Jewishness of the Tribulation period (Matthew 24:20; Revelation 7:4)
- fits the dispensational overview of Romans 11 (fulness...v.25 v. times...cp. Luke 21:24; Revelation 11:2)
- accommodates the hiatus between Daniel's 69th & 70th 'weeks'
- is in harmony with the precedent of the gap in Isaiah 61:1,2
- satisfies the different accents of 1 Thessalonians 4 & 5; 2 Thessalonians 2
- and distinguishes between Any-Moment (James 5:8) & Pre-Signalled phases (Matthew 24:27)

CHAPTER TWO: THERE'S A PLAN!

One Christmas my daughter Anna received a jigsaw as one of her presents. In my haste to remove all the fragments of discarded wrapping paper, I mistakenly threw away the part of the jigsaw's packaging that contained the picture showing what the jigsaw should finally look like. Without the picture to guide us, all the tiny pieces - many of them very similar – presented us with a real challenge. I'd like to suggest to you that watching news bulletins of world events, and trying to figure out what's going on in the world, is a bit like attempting to complete a jigsaw without the picture to show us what it should finally look like. It's my conviction, however, that it doesn't have to be like that, for the Bible gives us the final picture. If we can understand the picture – and that's sometimes no easy matter - we'll do better at making some sense of the jumble of world news items that pour in from around the globe. In this booklet, we're aiming to see if we can make out the Bible outlines of the shape of things to come.

To interpret Bible prophecy consistently, it's helpful to have some rules or guidelines. (See the full list used at the end of this e-book.) By that, I mean guidelines such as whenever a prediction has to do with strangely named places or peoples, we should arrive at the future identification of the places indicated by first establishing their geographical location at the time of writing. For example, as we'll see shortly, if 'the Romans' are indicated, then any future fulfilment would be expected to be in terms of some European bloc of countries, for that was principally where the Roman Empire held sway.

But more of that in a moment as we get into the Bible book of the prophet Daniel. The book of Daniel in the Old Testament of our Bibles is perhaps the major key to unlocking Bible prophecy. Some of us may remember from Sunday School days, the great stories from the first part of Daniel's writing. Stories like Daniel in the lions' den, and his three friends in the fiery furnace. But the book of Daniel also contains detailed and, at times, difficult prophecies. A lot of the predictions have already materialized, which gives us great confidence that the rest will also be fulfilled.

Perhaps the first clue we should pick up from Daniel's book is the fact that a large section of it was written in what, for Jews, was a foreign language. Chapters 2 through 7 were written in the international commercial language of the day, as opposed to what came before and what followed after, which was in Daniel's own native Jewish language. The predictions in the international language section relate to God's plans for the world in general; whereas in the remainder God reveals something of Israel's future. Even inside the international section of chapters 2 - 7 there's a pattern. The six chapters fall into two sets of three: with the second set being like a mirror image or reflection of the first. For example, the message of chapter 7 reflects, or repeats, the same message as chapter 2. And what God repeats must surely be of great importance. He draws our attention to this message for good reason for it was a prophecy about four great empires which were to dominate world history.

TOMORROW'S HEADLINES: THE FUTURE IN BIBLE PROPHECY

In chapter 2 they are pictured as four metals; but in chapter seven they are seen as four beasts. Let's start with chapter 2, where the Jewish captive, Daniel, is being asked to interpret the king of Babylon's dream:

> *"The king answered and said to Daniel ... 'Are you able to make known to me the dream which I have seen and its interpretation?'... 'You, O king, were looking and behold, there was a single great statue; that statue, which was large and of extraordinary splendor, was standing in front of you, and its appearance was awesome. The head of that statue was made of fine gold, its breast and its arms of silver, its belly and its thighs of bronze, its legs of iron, its feet partly of iron and partly of clay ... This was the dream; now we shall tell its interpretation before the king. You, O king, are the king of kings, to whom the God of heaven has given the kingdom, the power, the strength, and the glory; and wherever the sons of men dwell ... He has given them into your hand and has caused you to rule over them all. You are the head of gold. And after you there will arise another kingdom inferior to you, then another third kingdom of bronze, which will rule over all the earth.*
>
> *Then there will be a fourth kingdom as strong as iron; inasmuch as iron crushes and shatters all things, so, like iron that breaks in pieces, it will crush and break all these in pieces. And in that you saw the feet and toes, partly of potter's clay and partly of iron, it will be a divided kingdom; but it will have in it the toughness of*

iron, inasmuch as you saw the iron mixed with common clay. And as the toes of the feet were partly of iron and partly of pottery, so some of the kingdom will be strong and part of it will be brittle. And in that you saw the iron mixed with common clay, they will combine with one another in the seed of men; but they will not adhere to one another, even as iron does not combine with pottery. And in the days of those kings the God of heaven will set up a kingdom which will never be destroyed ..." (Daniel 2:26-44 NASB).

In this dramatic way, God unveiled, in the sixth century before Christ, his plan for the international world in general. Daniel names, or otherwise identifies for us, this succession of kingdoms or empires. There's no room for mere speculation. We've noted how Daniel has identified the first empire in the sequence as being the Babylonian. In chapter 8 (verses 20, 21), Daniel named in advance the two powers who did, in fact, come to succeed the Babylonians. As history has since confirmed, they were the Medo-Persian and the Grecian empires. History also allows us to identify the fourth empire as being plausibly the Roman Empire. This has been the view favoured by Bible scholars traditionally. More recently, an alternative view has been proposed that sees the fourth kingdom as the Islamic Caliphate. This was an empire that was centred on Babylon and lasted for some 1300 years. So, with the four empires of Babylon, Medo-Persia, Greece and Rome (or the Islamic Caliphate) in our minds, let's read the repeat of Daniel's message about them in chapter 7:

TOMORROW'S HEADLINES: THE FUTURE IN BIBLE PROPHECY

"These great beasts, which are four in number, are four kings who will arise from the earth. But the saints of the Highest One will receive the kingdom and possess the kingdom forever, for all ages to come. Then I desired to know the exact meaning of the fourth beast, which was different from all the others, exceedingly dreadful, with its teeth of iron and its claws of bronze, and which devoured, crushed, and trampled down the remainder with its feet, and the meaning of the ten horns that were on its head ... Thus he said: 'The fourth beast will be a fourth kingdom on the earth, which will be different from all the other kingdoms, and it will devour the whole earth and tread it down and crush it. As for the ten horns, out of this kingdom ten kings will arise..." (Daniel 7:17-24 NASB).

It's probably worth introducing here another helpful guideline for interpreting prophecy. And that's leaving the detailed interpretation of prophecy to the time when it's actually being fulfilled. In fact, there's nothing better than hindsight for establishing the true meaning of prophecy. You may think that something could then simply be made to fit, but a unique feature of Bible prophecy is how precisely detailed it is. When the prediction is fulfilled, it's unlikely we'll miss it. It fits like the missing piece in a jigsaw.

Which really brings us to this point about a confederacy of ten kingdoms. The glory that was Rome has come and gone as far as the history books are concerned. But the Roman, or European, empire has never yet existed (including in the fifth and sixth centuries) as a union of ten confederate kingdoms *at any one time.* There's good reason to see part of this prediction about the fourth empire as still awaiting fulfilment. Perhaps a parallel argument applies to the Islamic Caliphate. Remember what we were saying, that the Bible describes areas of the world that are to be involved in future events under the names they had at the time of writing or in terms of how they first appeared. The Roman Empire in history extended from Great Britain to Israel and included countries like Spain and Turkey and many more besides.

So, in effect, the Bible may either predict that a European bloc of countries or a Middle-eastern bloc of countries will come to assert itself and assume global influence - eclipsing even the influence the United States has now. We should also say that in all this Daniel's prophecy is fully supported by the prophetic visions of the apostle John in the book of Revelation - who even uses the same kind of picture language. So, on the basis of Daniel's repeated prophecy, we can either expect to see existing political reservations overcome so that some sort of federated union of sovereign states across Europe will at last emerge or otherwise a middle-eastern grouping influencing Europe as 'Eurabia' – and becoming a mighty military and political powerhouse in the world.

CHAPTER THREE: THE UNITED STATES OF EUROPE?

Perhaps we ought to begin this chapter by recapping. We've thought about the first event which believers on Jesus Christ are waiting for: his return for them. Contrary to some opinions, that won't signal the end of the world. The state of the world will continue to get worse once the salt of the earth - Christ's Church - has been removed from it. Trends which had already been developing will accelerate. One of the trends we have already begun to look at is the unification of Europe. Many see the Bible as predicting that a European bloc of countries will one day wield a global influence eclipsing even that of the United States currently. It will become a mighty military and political powerhouse as a federation of ten sovereign states. For a while, it won't appear quite like that. Others, more recently, have proposed another possibility: namely, that Islamic nations will once again come together as a Caliphate, as in the time of the Ottoman Empire. It's one of the golden rules of prophecy that we need to be prepared for complexities. Both the Bible books of Daniel and Revelation agree perfectly, however, in their gruesome portrayal of this empire as a monstrous beast with ten horns (Daniel 7:20, 24; Revelation 13:1; 17:3,12).

The horns, being ancient symbols of power, represent its ten confederate kings: the heads of sovereign states who have allied themselves with each other. We saw in the last chapter how the Bible prophet Daniel, around 600 BC, successfully anticipated the rise of the Persian and Greek empires - empires which did, indeed, emerge in the centuries that followed. Daniel didn't explicitly name the Roman Empire as the fourth kingdom he foresaw in his prophetic sweep forwards from the 6th century BC. Yet more than 2,500 years ago, Daniel did predict that, after the death of Jesus, a people would destroy Jerusalem and its rebuilt Temple (9:26b).

Historically, we know that the Romans carried out that destruction, so Daniel does, it might seem, identify Rome as a fourth kingdom. However, it turns out not to be quite that simple. That Roman army employed 'provincials', and so the actual destroyers of Jerusalem were Arabs, mainly Turks and Syrians. In fact, in dealing with the whole sweep of history right to its end, God, through prophets like Daniel, has never given any indication of a successor to either that Roman or Islamic empire. It seems that the emerging world-power to come - when fully developed in what the Bible calls 'the time of the end' - will be viewed by God in some sense as a continuation of the same empire. In other words, it will be a super-state stretching very roughly over the same geographical area as it once covered historically.

Taking the Roman option first, it's an idea that may take a little getting used to, but it's by no means far-fetched. After all, it's been attempted many times already, down through the centuries, by leaders like Charlemagne, Otto the Great, Napoleon Bonaparte and, more recently, by Mussolini. In fact, speaking of attempts to resurrect (in effect) the old Roman Empire, it was Winston Churchill who said: "We must build a kind of United States of Europe" (Zurich). That was back in 1946. As we've said, more than 2,500 years ago, the Bible predicted that, after the death of Jesus, the people of a still future prince would destroy Jerusalem and its Temple. Since, historically, the Romans carried out that destruction, we have to conclude that the coming world leader will be associated with people from roughly the same area over which Rome once held sway. As for the way being prepared for his emergence, it's interesting to note that, as long ago as 1957, Paul Henri Spaak, the Secretary General of N.A.T.O., speaking of the greatest need in Europe - said, "We do not want another committee ... what we want is a man of sufficient stature to hold the allegiance of all people ... if such a man appeared, were he god or devil, we would give our authority to him." This latter-day Caesar has many titles in the Bible, but he's most popularly referred to as 'the Antichrist'.

It never seemed possible back in the mid-1980s, but within a few years the Soviet Union had disintegrated, Germany had reunited, and the Warsaw Pact had dissolved. The political landscape of Europe is now set for much more change. Europe is destined to be a major player in the new world order. In an interview in Paris in 1989, Mikhail Gorbachev echoed words spoken thirty years earlier by Charles De Gaulle when he spoke of a Europe united "from the Atlantic to the Ural Mountains". The rhetoric of statesmen is one thing; the means to achieve it, however, has eluded many. Statesmen and soldiers have dreamt of a greater Europe for centuries. Hitler attempted it by force, plunging the continent - and the world - into a devastating war. Others, like Jacques Delors, work away quietly, using behind-the-scenes diplomacy. Ever since the Second World War, Europe has been trying hard to unite. In 1948, seventeen European countries banded together to give effect to the Marshall Plan. Ten years later, in 1958, six countries - Belgium, France, Italy, Luxembourg, the Netherlands and West Germany - came together to form a group known as the European Community with its parliament and court of justice in Brussels. In 1986, the EEC officially adopted the goal of a politically unified Europe. In 1992 tariffs and trade quotas were eliminated to help this European bloc of countries function more easily as a single community of cooperating countries.

Then the 1990s saw the beginning of the end of the old East-West divide across Europe. The year 2002 brought the introduction of a common currency across 'euro land'. Progress may seem slow, but when we review it like that, over the sweep of decades, it's moving overall in exactly the direction the Bible says it will go - the direction of a unified Europe. Those who don't know the God of the Bible ought to be amazed that trends of the past century sit comfortably with predictions made in the Bible two and a half thousand years ago! The fact remains that it's now not hard to imagine Europe finally becoming a confederation of sovereign states. But the issue of individual national sovereignty continues to bedevil moves to fully unify Europe today. Perhaps, it will always remain a problem, for the Bible describes this final European super-state as:

> *"... partly of potter's clay and partly of iron, it will be a divided kingdom; but it will have in it the toughness of iron, inasmuch as you saw the iron mixed with common clay. And as the toes of the feet were partly of iron and partly of pottery, so some of the kingdom will be strong and part of it will be brittle. And in that you saw the iron mixed with common clay, they will combine with one another in the seed of men; but they will not adhere*

to one another, even as iron does not combine with pottery" (Daniel 2:40-43 NASB).

The Bible's prediction could well be understood as indicating that the union of states across Europe will always be a brittle one, constantly subject to the strains of nationalism. We have recently seen devastating evidence of nationalism as a disintegrating factor on the continent of Europe. Be that as it may, let's remind ourselves that the Gentile superpower with control of the land of Israel when Christ was born was the Roman Empire which spread from Great Britain to Israel and included Spain and Asia Minor (Turkey). History is destined to repeat itself when Christ, the Messiah, returns. This brings us to another of the golden rules for understanding Bible prophecy: we need to be aware of the time perspective.

Statements of prophecy and predicted events that seem to flow one into the other can sometimes be widely separated in actual time as far as their fulfilment is concerned. In that respect, it's a bit like adjacent-looking mountain ranges which, on closer inspection, turn out to have huge valleys between them. Just as two summits in a mountain range look to be adjacent and connected from a distance, so Christ's two advents at a time of Roman domination of the holy land appear at times in the Bible to be without an intervening 'valley' of at least 2,000 years. Two thousand years have run their course since Christ first came at a time when Rome held sway. When he returns to earth a second time (to complete the second phase of his Second Advent), either a European / Roman empire - or a Middle-eastern / Islamic empire - as the Bible stills views it will once again be exerting itself against Israel, and in many ways will be dominating events as they unfold in the Middle East. Its leader:

> *"... will give great honor to those who acknowledge him, and he will cause them to rule over the many, and will parcel out land for a price ... he will enter countries, overflow them, and pass through. He will also enter the Beautiful Land* [that's Daniel's code for Israel], *and many countries will fall"* (Daniel 11:39-41 NASB).

The threats and dangers of today will pave the way for a strong leader. Recession, nationalism, environmental disaster, ethnic tension, religious intolerance and a deepening crisis in the Middle East will propel a leader out of the shadows. Napoleon came to power in France in the confusion of the Revolution. Hitler was hailed as the man to lift Germany out of economic and psychological depression after its stinging defeat in the First World War. Lenin and Stalin rode to power on the back of mass discontentment. Someone far more powerful is waiting his moment. He'll make his mark by negotiating peace on Israel's borders. Illustrious American presidents and diplomats have beaten a trail to the Middle East, and to Jerusalem especially, in search of that elusive peace accord between Israel and its neighbours. Progress seemed to have been made by Jimmy Carter when he managed to bring Egypt and Israel together, but it ended with Egypt being ostracized and Sadat assassinated. Clinton seemed to make progress at Oslo with a land for peace plan between Israel and the Palestinians, but that, too, has since stalled. This is one problem America won't crack; but Europe will.* That much is clear from Daniel's prophecy: *"the people of the prince who is to* *come will destroy the city and the sanctuary ... And he will make a firm covenant with the many for one 'seven'"* (Daniel 9:26-27).

It was the Roman people who destroyed Jerusalem and its Temple in 70 AD. Since, historically, the Romans carried out that destruction - and they are described as 'the people of the prince' – it's defensible to conclude that the coming world leader will be associated with people from roughly the same area over which Rome once held sway. Towards the end of history, the Bible says a critical seven-year period begins when the head of a federal Europe signs an historic peace deal for Israel. What a leader he'll be seen to be - unifying Europe and making peace in the Middle East!

Let me, in closing this chapter, remind you of the basis for the alternative view. It was indeed the Roman general, Titus, who in AD70 was associated with the destruction of the Jerusalem temple. The complicating aspect is this: his troops were not crack European legions, but were drawn from Middle Eastern peoples, those who traditionally had a hatred for the Jews. Josephus records that they took delight in far exceeding Titus' orders when destroying the temple. This does allow for the alternative scenario that a revived caliphate may be in view in Daniel, one possibly even headed by an Islamic Antichrist!

* Some commentators would grossly extend the borders of the 'revived Roman Empire' away beyond those of the historical Roman Empire, so as to embrace America. This, however, seems to go against the 6th 'key' or 'golden rule' we are employing in this study book.

CHAPTER FOUR: PROMISES, PROMISES!

Among the most important things that may be said by married men and women are the words, "I do ... I will", on their wedding day. These words make a solemn, binding promise and emphasize marriage as a covenant. In the Bible, there are four major occasions when God says "I will". They're so major that they give shape to world history and to God's programme of events. The stunning thing about them is that all four of them involve Israel. Bible predictions are amazing for the prominent place given over to Israel; it's a place which is out of all proportion to her size. Just as we have previously established the rise of Europe as a major feature of biblical prophecy, we now need to see the wide Bible underpinning for a re-emergent Israel. It's another key to Bible prophecy that we should have regard to whole Bible perspectives. We need to strenuously guard against the danger of plucking texts out of context. On the first of these four times when God said "I will", he was speaking to Abraham. Look at the number of times he repeats, "I will" in the following quote from the beginning of Genesis chapter 12:

> *"Now the LORD said to Abram, 'Go forth from your country, and from your relatives and from your father's house, to the land which **I will** show you; and **I will** make you a great nation, and **I will** bless you, and make your name great; and so you shall be a blessing; and **I will** bless those who bless you, and the one who curses you*

I will *curse. And in you all the families of the earth shall be blessed'"* (Genesis 12:1-3 NASB).

God's "I will" covenant promise to Abraham included that:

- Abraham's name would be great;
- a great nation would come from him;
- all the families of the earth would be blessed;
- the land of Palestine would be given to him and to his seed;
- the multitude of his seed would be as the dust of the earth;
- whoever blessed or cursed him would themselves be blessed or cursed;
- he would be the father of many nations;
- kings would proceed from him;
- and the covenant would be 'an everlasting covenant';
- with the land of Canaan as 'an everlasting possession'.
- It also included the promise that God would be a God to him and to his seed;
- his seed would possess the gate of its enemies;
- and in his seed all the nations of the earth would be blessed.

That all adds up to quite a list, doesn't it? The list included personal, national and universal blessings. Some things were personal to Abraham, like his name would become great. Some aspects of the promise were national, relating to the nation of Israel which would descend from Abraham - like how theirs was to be the land of Palestine. Other aspects of this great promise were universal, as in every nation becoming blessed through his descendants. Through Abraham, God promised Israel a land and a seed (Genesis 13:15): *"I will give [the land] ... to your descendants forever."*

The plain, unconditional nature of God's "I will" covenant to Abraham seems to promise Israel permanent existence as well as the ultimate possession of their land. As far as events in the Middle East are concerned, we're still watching this space. But the various parts of God's promise to Abraham didn't even begin to be fulfilled right away. First of all, there was a delay of 25 years before Abraham's wife Sarah even gave birth to their special son, Isaac. Hundreds of years rolled by before Moses prepared the Israelite people to set foot in their promised land. Perhaps on the brink of that delayed entry, and facing hostile occupants, they began to have their own doubts about God's promise to Abraham. But when Moses spoke to them, his tone was reassuring, and his words were God's words. When Moses said "He will", it was the same as God directly saying, "I will".

> *"If your outcasts are at the ends of the earth, from there the LORD your God will gather you, and from there **He will** bring you back. And the LORD your **God will** bring you into the land which your fathers possessed, and you shall possess it; and **He will** prosper you and multiply you more than your fathers. Moreover the LORD your **God will** circumcise your heart and the heart of your descendants, to love the LORD your God with all your heart and with all your soul, in order that you may live ... And you shall again obey the LORD, and observe all His commandments which I command*

you today" (Deuteronomy 30:1-10 NASB, the so-called 'Palestinian covenant').

In these clear, resounding terms, God, through Moses, reaffirmed Israel's title deed to the land of promise. In fact, the matter of their possession of the land is emphasized more than ever here. Yet what's really impressive is how their anticipated disobedience - their repeated disobedience - would not be allowed to derail God's long-term plans for them in the land he'd promised to them. God kept his promise when he brought them back from captivity in Babylon, but there's more than that here: there's talk of a future re-gathering from worldwide dispersion (from 'the ends of the earth'), and there's mention of national conversion (when they receive 'a circumcised heart'); all that before obtaining full possession of the land and its blessings. So, for Israel, the best is still to come.

There are those who would query that, of course. It's become fashionable to interpret the promises God made to Israel as not being literal promises for them, but as being fulfilled through Christ's Church in some sort of spiritual way today. However, this book presents and attempts to justify the 'pre-Millennial view' *. This sees Christ completing the second stage of his Second Advent prior to a literal reign on earth for a thousand years. Some used to think we were already living in the biblical Millennium inasmuch as society, as they viewed it, was becoming increasingly 'Christianized'. Ever since the Second World War in the last century that view has been scarcely credible. However, some do view Christ as head of the Church as currently fulfilling the prediction of his Millennial rule. The evidence against that view is very impressive, however, as we continue to make our way through God's four main "I will" promises. The next one we come to was spoken to David, the king of Israel around 1,000 BC:

> *"'Thus says the LORD of hosts, "I took you from the pasture, from following the sheep, that you should be ruler over My people Israel. And I have been with you wherever you have gone and have cut off all your enemies from before you; and **I will** make you a great name ... **I will** also appoint a place for My people Israel and will plant them, that they may live in their own place and not be disturbed again ... and **I will** give you rest from all your enemies.*

> *"'The LORD also declares to you that **the LORD will** make a house for you. When your days are complete ... **I will** raise up your descendant after you, who will come forth from you, and **I will** establish his kingdom. He shall build a house for My name, and **I will** establish the throne of his kingdom forever. **I will** be a father to him and he will be a son to Me; when he commits iniquity, **I will** correct him ... but My lovingkindness shall not depart from him, as I took it away from Saul, whom I removed from before you. And your house and your kingdom shall endure before Me forever; your throne shall be established forever'"* (2 Samuel 7:8-16 NASB, the so-called 'Davidic covenant').

The major terms of this promise have to do with a house, a kingdom and a throne. Its 'sure' provisions (see Isaiah 55) are that:

- David is to have a child, a successor who will build the temple;

TOMORROW'S HEADLINES: THE FUTURE IN BIBLE PROPHECY

- and the throne of his kingdom will be established forever;
- it will not be taken away, even if he sins.

And if one word struck you from that reading a moment ago, I think it ought to have been 'forever'. David's house, throne and kingdom were to be established for ever. But is this promise really satisfied by the household of faith now, and Christ's heavenly throne, as some suggest? Israel certainly interpreted the 'kingdom' as a future, earthly, national kingdom. The New Testament makes 59 references to David, but none of them are fully fulfilled in terms of Christ's present reign. God the Father's throne is not 'the throne of David' (Luke 1:31-33). The Bible elsewhere makes clear mention of a future period of Jewish blessing after a period of Gentile blessing (Acts 15:16-17; Romans 11:27). So we come back to the view that these are literal promises for Israel. So, finally, we come to the fourth "I will" promise, recognizable to us, I'm sure, as the 'new covenant':

> *"Behold, days are coming,"* declares the LORD [through Jeremiah, the prophet], *"when **I will** make a new covenant with the house of Israel and with the house of Judah, not like the covenant which I made with their fathers in the day I took them by the hand to bring them out of the land of Egypt ...* [that was the 'old covenant'] *But this is the covenant which I will make with the house of Israel after those days,"* declares the LORD, *"**I will** put My law within them, and on their heart **I will** write it; and **I will** be their God, and they shall be My people. And they shall not teach again,*

*each man his neighbor and each man his brother, saying, 'Know the LORD,' for they shall all know Me, from the least of them to the greatest of them," declares the LORD, "for **I will** forgive their iniquity, and their sin **I will** remember no more"* (Jeremiah 31:31-34 NASB).

This new covenant, which is also applied to believers on the Lord Jesus Christ later in the Bible (Hebrews 10:15,16), separately guarantees that Israel will be re-gathered, converted, and have her sins removed as the basis for the future restoration of all her blessings in her land, after Christ's second coming (Romans 11:26-27). All we've seen in these four great "I will" promises might be summed up as:

- a nation forever
- a land forever
- a king forever
- a throne forever
- a kingdom forever
- a new covenant and
- lasting blessings.

These seven features give us clear insight into how to interpret Bible prophecy. A golden rule is to follow an essentially literal approach. Bible prophecies are bound up with God's covenants. The covenants themselves are prophetic and give an absolute cast-iron guarantee of Israel's future. We can only properly understand these 4 covenants in a literal way as still relating to Israel in the future. So, it should be very clear that the Bible predicts a future for Israel in her own land.

* Thiessen has shown that the early 'church fathers' (as well as the writers of the New Testament) "held not only the pre-millennial view of Christ's coming, but also regarded that coming as imminent". This view did not originate with J.N. Darby in the early 19th century as some think, although he did systematize its teaching.

CHAPTER FIVE: A NEW EXODUS & A BORN-AGAIN ISRAEL

God isn't finished with Israel yet. We're indebted to the apostle Paul for making that very clear. In his letter to the Romans, he begins chapter eleven by repeating, *"God has not rejected his people"*. He concedes a temporary, purposeful rejection; but not a final, absolute one. For he argues that: *"if their rejection is the reconciliation of the world, what will their acceptance be but life from the dead?"* (11:15).

He then explains further in verse 25 that a partial hardening has happened to Israel until the fullness of the Gentiles has come in. After God has shown favour to Gentiles - and what greater favour could there be than the spread of the Gospel worldwide - he will once more show mercy to Israel. In support, Paul quotes the prophet Isaiah: *"A deliverer will come from Zion. He will ... take away their sins"*. It was these considerations that drew from the apostle Paul the breathless admiration: *"Oh, the depth of the riches both of the wisdom and knowledge of God!"* (v.33). Why has God put so much prophecy in the Bible? For one thing, to remind us that he is sovereign. The future belongs to him. Surely it has the effect of keeping us humble when we realize that our times truly are in his hand. It ought to bring us to our knees in worship for the awesome divine wisdom displayed through God's plan of salvation for Jew and Gentile. There have been times in history when Israel seemed down and out. In the times

TOMORROW'S HEADLINES: THE FUTURE IN BIBLE PROPHECY

of the Pharaohs, their prospects might have seemed dim to any human observer. But God flexed his muscles on behalf of this people, and *"with an outstretched arm"*, as the Bible records, he brought them out. Theirs was a wonderful Exodus through the Red Sea and on towards the land God had long before promised to their ancestor, Abraham.

Once again little Israel is on the ropes. She has few, if any, friends in the Middle East. Many forecast again that her prospects are dim. But through the Bible prophet, Ezekiel, God sends out a different message. What's more, there's an interesting pattern to God's message through Ezekiel - a pattern which invites us to make comparisons with what happened before when God brought them out from under Pharaoh. Just as God once brought Israel out of Egypt to bring them into their own land, God has made promise to Ezekiel about a future exodus. At a time in history when the Babylonians had just finished reducing Jerusalem to rubble, God made this promise:

> *"For I will take you from the nations, gather you from all the lands, and bring you into your own land ... Moreover, I will give you a new heart and put a new spirit within you ... And I will put My Spirit within you and cause you to ... observe My ordinances. And you will live in the land that I gave to your forefathers; so you will be My people, and I will be your God"* (Ezekiel 36:24-28 NASB).

When God brought Israel out of Egypt, it had been a new start for the nation, like a new birth. But even that pales in significance alongside the future vision of a nation being reborn, truly receiving *life from the dead,* in Paul's words. That was the vision Ezekiel received. For God gave his prophet a vision of a valley:

> *"... and it was full of bones ... He said to me, "Prophesy over these bones, and say to them, 'O dry bones, hear the word of the LORD.' Thus says the Lord GOD to these bones, 'Behold, I will cause breath to enter you that you may come to life. And I will put sinews on you, make flesh grow back on you, cover you with skin, and put breath in you that you may come alive; and you will know that I am the LORD.'" So I prophesied as I was commanded; and as I prophesied, there was a noise, and behold, a rattling; and the bones came together, bone to its bone. And I looked, and behold, sinews were on them, and flesh grew, and skin covered them; but there was no breath in them. Then He said to me, "Prophesy to the breath, prophesy, son of man, and say to the breath, 'Thus says the Lord GOD, "Come from the four winds, O breath, and breathe on these slain, that they come to life." So I prophesied as He commanded me, and the breath came into them, and they came to life, and stood on their feet, an exceedingly great army. Then He said to me, "Son of man, these bones are the whole house of Israel"'* (Ezekiel 37:1-11 NASB).

Today Israel is partially re-gathered into its ancient homeland. But the time is still to come when the whole of Israel will be re-gathered into that land. A nation which has been 'reborn' will finally recognize that its Deliverer, its Messiah, is none other than Jesus the Nazarene. Have you ever wondered why the words of

Isaiah chapter 53 are in the past tense? *"We ourselves esteemed Him stricken, smitten of God, and afflicted. But He was pierced through for our transgressions ..."* (vv.4,5).

It's because they belong in the mouth of Jews in a future day when they look back and finally realize what it was that their forefathers did at the cross of Jesus Christ. While they held him to be an imposter and blasphemer, they discerned him being stricken by God at that time for his perceived sin; but at this future date we are thinking about, aghast, they suddenly realize that, in actual fact, Jesus had been pierced for their sins! That will be saving faith for Israel in the future. This is when those words in Romans 11:26 will be fulfilled: *"A deliverer will come from Zion. He will ... take away their sins".*

Some take issue with the fact that Christ-hating Jews of today will ever be converted. But wasn't that the case with Saul of Tarsus? How can we underestimate the grace of God, when we, too, merited only the judgement of God? We've already seen how four major covenants in the Old Testament can never be satisfied unless God takes up dealings once more with his ancient people. The reason we have already referred twice to Paul's letter to the Romans is because that's where we see the interlocking of God's purposes for Jew and Gentile explained side by side. We've been following Ezekiel's parallel with Israel's historical exodus from Egypt. After freeing his people long ago, God instructed them to build a house or sanctuary for him so that he might live among them. From Exodus chapter 25 onwards we read of the details of the historical sanctuary known as the tabernacle. In the future, too, after the redemption of his people, God once again instructs them to build him a house or sanctuary. In chapter 43 God says to Ezekiel:

> *"... this is the place of My throne and the place of the soles of My feet, where I will dwell among the sons of Israel forever ... As for you, son of man, describe the temple to the house of Israel, that they may be ashamed of their iniquities; and let them measure the plan'* (Ezekiel 43:7-10 NASB).

History's certainly going to repeat itself. In Exodus chapter 40 (v.35), when Moses had supervised everything being built to God's satisfaction, there was a description given (in Exodus 40:34) of how God's glory filled the tabernacle. So with Ezekiel, the same pattern continues, for Ezekiel says, *"the Spirit lifted me up and brought me into the inner court; and behold, the glory of the LORD filled the house"* (Ezekiel 43:5 NASB).

So far, the pattern has included God delivering his people; instructing them to build him a sanctuary or temple; and then God himself coming to take up residence in it as shown by the presence of a visible glory. But there's more! Historically, when God gave details of his sanctuary which they were to build for him, along with the construction details, he included information about the clothing of the priests. In Ezekiel, he does the same thing again in relation to worship in the future temple. Here are to be its 'operating instructions':

> *"The Levitical priests, the sons of Zadok, who kept charge of My sanctuary when the sons of Israel went astray from Me, shall come near to Me to minister to*

Me; and they shall stand before Me to offer Me the fat and the blood," declares the Lord GOD. They shall enter My sanctuary; they shall come near to My table to minister to Me and keep My charge. And it shall be that when they enter at the gates of the inner court, they shall be clothed with linen garments; and wool shall not be on them while they are ministering in the gates of the inner court and in the house. Linen turbans shall be on their heads, and linen undergarments shall be on their loins; they shall not gird themselves with anything which makes them sweat" (Ezekiel 44:15-18 NASB).

Here again objections may be raised regarding the apparent return to animal sacrifices. A literal reading of this section certainly demands a return to animal sacrifices. But how can this be realistic after Christ's once for all sacrifice has taken place? Might it not be that these future sacrifices are intended to look back to the only sacrifice of real worth in the same way as they once pointed forward to it? What had previously taken place in ignorance will be done again in the future with real insight. To complete the parallel between the historical exodus and this prophesied exodus, Ezekiel finally describes the land of Israel being divided up between the tribes: *"so you shall divide this land among yourselves according to the tribes of Israel"* (Ezekiel 47:21 NASB). This is just as can be found earlier in the Book of Numbers. With Paul, we say again: *Oh, the depth of the riches both of the wisdom and knowledge of God!*

CHAPTER SIX: WAR AND PEACE

If the survival of Israel's identity right down to the present day is remarkable, then it's all the more remarkable that her astonishing story is set to continue. Through Bible prophecy, God spelled out His plans for Israel long ago - and they are not finished yet. Over a hundred years ago there was little obvious sign of these Biblical predictions ever materializing. But what a difference the past hundred years has made! We need only remind ourselves how, after centuries of dispersion and homelessness, a Zionist society was founded in the nineteenth century in order to promote the idea of Jews resettling in the land of Palestine. Such a resettling, or re-gathering, was something different Bible prophets - like Isaiah and Ezekiel - had predicted time and time again in their writings.

In 1897, Theodor Herzl organised the first Zionist Congress. He claimed even then to have effectively established the Jewish state. Then a man by the name of Eliezer Ben Yehuda brought about a revival of the old Hebrew language. Following that, in November 1917, came the 'Balfour Declaration' which pledged support for the Jewish people in finding a national home once again in Palestine. As the years passed, the terrible events of the holocaust evoked sympathy for the Jews, and Palestine became an issue of world concern. This all led to the 1947 United Nations resolution, which split Palestine into a Jewish and an Arab state. The following year David Ben-Gurion proclaimed Israel's independence. Israel was back! Back in their land; back speaking their historical language; and back reading their ancient Scriptures, courtesy of the famous find of the Dead Sea scrolls in 1947. This recognition of the State of Israel in 1948 was surely a crucial step in the realization of the biblical prediction that there would once more be a re-emergent, re-gathered Israel - available as a major player at *the time of the end,* as the Bible styles it.

The years since 1948 have certainly been difficult for Israel - and for their neighbours. They were never expected to be easy. Days before Israel's formal recognition, a veiled figure dressed as an Arab entered the residence of King Abdullah of Jordan. Golda Meir, who would shortly become Israel's prime minister, was that secretive visitor - coming in what would prove to be a failed attempt to find a way for Jews and Arabs to get along. The story of Jew and Arab since then has been a story of war and peace - and it has to be said that atrocities have been committed on both sides.

In 1967 war broke out, the "6-Day War". The outcome of that war which seemed most important to many was that it left the Temple Mount under Israeli control. Six more years of uneasy peace erupted again in the Yom Kippur War of 1973. Following that, Henry Kissinger began his shuttle diplomacy. The result was a cease-fire between Israel and Egypt, but still not lasting peace in the Middle East. Then Egypt's President, Anwar Sadat, made an historic trip to Jerusalem in November 1977 for face to face talks with Menachem Begin. This bold move led to the Camp David Peace Accord brokered by US President Jimmy Carter. Egypt might have become the first Arab nation to formally acknowledge Israel's right to exist as a nation, but it cost

Sadat his life, mown down by an assassin. After further war in 1982 when Israel invaded Lebanon, it seemed that the restraint of Israel during the Gulf War of 1991 - together with the goodwill engendered then between the US and many Arab states - might at last be set to deliver on the peace process.

A peace deal based on mutual recognition of the state of Israel and the PLO was negotiated in Oslo, and Bill Clinton presided over a historic handshake between Palestinian leader Yasser Arafat and Israel's Rabin in 1993. Then Rabin, too, was assassinated; and later the process seemed to grind to a halt in the year 2000. As it stands now, the process depends on joint Israeli/Palestinian negotiation to establish the boundaries of a Palestinian state. They need to agree on the future of Jerusalem, on the right of Palestinian refugees to return to Israel, and on the presence of Jewish settlements in the occupied territories. But overall, there can be no doubt that God's behind the return of Jews to their ancient land. Their terrible crime in crucifying the Messiah did indeed bring about an interruption in his dealings with them. But since then, through the trial and discipline of hard times - which will get far worse before they are better - Israel is being prepared once again to meet the same Messiah she rejected at his first advent.

We have been looking back in order to look forward. In a sense that's what the prophet Daniel was doing in his day. It was while he was an exile in Babylon, held captive there during the time when the Babylonians had destroyed Jerusalem and deported the Jews from their homeland. One day as Daniel was reading the book of the prophet Jeremiah (Daniel 9:2), he saw something there he had not understood before. God had actually decreed that their current captivity would last 70 years. And the 70 years were nearly up, that was what excited Daniel. At once he bowed his head in a wonderful prayer of confession recorded in chapter 9 of his book. God answered his appeal for forgiveness on behalf of his people. Looking back, Daniel was made to realize that God had imposed 70 years exile - 70 years of enforced rest on the land of Israel because for the past 490 years his people had failed to observe the command of allowing the land to rest fallow every seventh year (2 Chronicles 36:21).

But, looking forward, God gave Daniel a vision of 490 years to come. In the same way as the 490 years that were past had been built up from 70 groups of seven years, in each of which the land had not enjoyed its 'sabbath'; so the 490 years that now stretched ahead in God's programme for Israel were divided up - in the same way - as 70 groups of 'sevens'. The 'seventy sevens' are usually translated as 'seventy weeks' in our Bibles, but the word really means 'seven' and the context shows it's seven years - or a 'week of years', if you like. Here then is the vision God gave to Daniel (9:24-27):

> *"Seventy weeks have been decreed for your people and your holy city, to finish the transgression, to make an end of sin, to make atonement for iniquity, to bring in everlasting righteousness, to seal up vision and prophecy, and to anoint the most holy place."*

Let's just interrupt here to say that this obviously hasn't happened yet as far as Israel is concerned. That's the first clue that there's a future element here. So the entire 490 years weren't consecutive from that time. The first question is: 'when did they begin?' Verse 25 answers that: *"So you are to know and discern that from the issuing of a decree to restore and rebuild Jerusalem until Messiah the Prince there will be seven weeks and sixty-two weeks ..."* This decree to restore Jerusalem was the one which was later given in 444 BC by Artaxerxes in the 20th year of his reign. The record of the giving of this decree to rebuild the city of Jerusalem can be found in the Bible book of Nehemiah (2:1,5): *"Then **after** ... the Messiah will be cut off and have nothing."*

The Messiah being 'cut off' refers to the crucifixion of Jesus Christ. While it was to take place 'after' the completion of the 69 weeks, the wording avoided saying that it was 'during' the 70th week (indicating a gap, and so a second pointer to a future element). When the best historical dates are used for Artaxerxes' decree and for the death of Jesus, it can indeed be shown that there are precisely '69 weeks' between them.* But when the Jews crucified Jesus, the Messiah whom God had sent, it was as though Daniel's clock stopped ticking. In other words, the final seven years of the prophecy, the '70th week', hasn't happened yet. To see that, listen to the remainder of Daniel's vision: *"... and the people of the prince who is to come will destroy the city and the sanctuary ... even to the end there will be war ... And he will make a firm covenant with the many for one week."*

History tells us that it was the Roman people under Titus who destroyed the temple at Jerusalem in AD 70, which means that 'the prince who is [still] to come' must be a Roman prince - in other words a European leader (see an earlier caveat in chapter 3). Daniel wrote *"even to the end there will be war"* (a third clue pointing us to fulfilment at the time of the end). The Middle East was always predicted to stay troubled towards the time of

TOMORROW'S HEADLINES: THE FUTURE IN BIBLE PROPHECY

the end especially. Daniel's clock only seems to start ticking again when this leader, who comes to dominate the world, signs a seven-year deal which will aim to guarantee the security of Israel's borders. Someone's coming who will succeed where Kissinger, Carter, Baker, Clinton, Bush, Blair & co have all failed. But lasting peace will have to wait for none other than the Lord Jesus Christ. The Bible says he's still to come as a deliverer to Zion. He, and no-one else, can bring true peace to Jerusalem!

* From 444 BC to 33 AD (the best date for the crucifixion), there are 476 years (not 477 due to the difference between 1 BC & 1 AD being only 1 year. 69 'weeks' are 69x7=483 years (of 360 days – see Revelation where three and a half years is equivalent to 1,260 days) which is equivalent to 476 solar years of just over 365 days each.

APPENDIX TO CHAPTER 6
Summary of points supporting the fact that Daniel's '70th week' is still future:

- the 6 things of v.24 are not already accomplished nationally
- Messiah was cut off 'after' 7+62 weeks, but not 'during' the 70th
- the subject of v.27 is the Roman prince of v.26, and not Christ
- Christ would never break a covenant
- the 'ending of sacrifice' is not Christ's death
- Jews sacrificed animals until AD 70
- v.27 not fully fulfilled historically since in Matthew 24:15 the Lord spoke of it still to happen
- nor did Christ return in AD 70
- the strong correlation between the person of Daniel 9:27 & Revelation 12 & 13 would otherwise be denied whereas Daniel 9:27b events match Revelation's description of the future 3.5 years of the special Tribulation period.

CHAPTER SEVEN: THE THIRD TEMPLE PROJECT

In the sixth century BC a small minority of Jews returned to Israel and began to rebuild the temple at Jerusalem that had been demolished decades earlier by the invading superpower which had deported them to captivity. That rebuilding project, eventually led to the construction of what's often referred to as the Second Temple. Obviously, the original temple built by King Solomon was the first. The building of the Second Temple turned out to be a matter of some political controversy due to opposition from settlers. The Bible books of Ezra and Nehemiah record for us the stop-go nature of that building project. But all traces of that temple were destroyed in the first century of our era. It's now more than 19 centuries since Israel has had its own temple. For the past thirteen centuries, the Islamic faith has dominated the Old City of Jerusalem and the Temple Mount.

But things changed in 1967. During the Six-Day War, Israel captured the Old City of Jerusalem, and gained control once more over their ancient capital. In an act of restraint - so as to avoid any holy war - the Israeli government has refused to modify any of the holy sites on Temple Mount. Buildings sacred to the Islamic faith - the El-Aqsa mosque and the Dome of the Rock - stand on a platform Herod the Great built 2,000 years ago for Israel's temple. Muslims still administer the Temple Mount, but many Jews - a growing number - want to rebuild their temple in Israel. In a 1983 newspaper poll, eighteen percent of Israelis felt that the time was right to rebuild the temple. In 1989, Israel's Ministry of Religious Affairs hosted a Conference of Temple Research. Groups have formed to prepare the articles of clothing and the utensils that would be needed for a rebuilt temple. These items are on display in a museum at the Temple Institute in Jerusalem.

In a booklet explaining their purpose, the Temple Institute shows its longing for a rebuilt temple, when it says: 'The dream of rebuilding the Temple spans 50 generations of Jews, five continents and innumerable seas and oceans ... With God's help we will soon be able to rebuild the Temple on its holy mountain in Jerusalem, ushering in an era of peace and understanding, love and kindness, when 'God will be king over all the earth, in that day God will be one and his name will be one'.'

Work goes on to breed the red heifer (see Numbers 19) and to prepare other necessary articles and clothing for a rebuilt temple. So a small minority of Jews are making serious preparations to rebuild the temple and resume its worship. But will a temple realistically ever be built again on land already occupied by Muslim mosques and shrines? Will there be a third temple? The apostle Paul answers:

> *"Let no one in any way deceive you, for it - the day of the Lord [4] - will not come unless the apostasy comes first, [1] and the man of lawlessness is revealed, the son of destruction, who opposes and exalts himself above every so-called god or object of worship, so that he takes his seat in the temple of God, displaying himself as being God. Do you not remember that while I was still with you, I was telling you these things? And you know what restrains*

TOMORROW'S HEADLINES: THE FUTURE IN BIBLE PROPHECY

him now, so that in his time he may be revealed. For the mystery of lawlessness is already at work; only he who now restrains will do so until he is taken out of the way [lit. 'until out of the midst he appears']. *And then that lawless one will be revealed* [2] *whom the Lord will slay with the breath of His mouth and bring to an end by the appearance of His coming;* [3] *that is, the one whose coming is in accord with the activity of Satan, with all power and signs and false wonders, and with all the deception of wickedness for those who perish, because they did not receive the love of the truth so as to be saved"* (2 Thessalonians 2:1-10 NASB).

Notice the sequence of events 1-4. Paul declares the Great Tribulation, or more specifically the Day of the Lord which terminates it, would not overtake them. Christ's Church is not in any danger of passing through the Great Tribulation (see also 1 Thessalonians 5:9). To believe the Church passes through the Great Tribulation, as some do, is to jumble up this biblically given sequence*. Paul writes of a future temple which will be commandeered by a sinister figure he describes as the lawless one. That's a striking way of describing this future world leader. For we would expect lawlessness to be opposed by the power of the state (Romans 13). And there had been times when the apostle Paul himself had reason to be thankful for the restraint of law as wielded by the Roman Empire (Acts 18:12-16). But if a European power bloc, the modern geographical equivalent of the Roman Empire of history, were to gain the ascendancy in world affairs at the time of the end, we might begin to make sense of Paul's words here. Indeed, this would be good reason for Paul appearing to be more than a little cryptic. It certainly would have been prudent for him not to talk too openly about the removal of the restraining power of a Roman state! But at some future point in time, with Satanic timing, this lawless one appears on the scene *out of the midst* of a superpower which up till then has generally been a restraining influence. His anti-social, anti-law and anti-God agenda will at once be apparent. Not that such things aren't around already in the undercurrents of self-centred materialism and godless ideologies and moral permissiveness - but they are clearly destined to become much worse. But we had best not lose sight of what we were saying - about a rebuilt temple, a third Jerusalem Temple.

The apostle Paul's view of the future assumes there will be one - that was the main point. But before the temple can be rebuilt, its exact former location will need to be determined, presumably by archaeological excavations - something Arabs in Jerusalem seem unlikely to permit. In 1990, the mere rumour of a group of Jews planning to lay a foundation stone was enough to bring out thousands of angry demonstrators. It has been suggested (via an article in Biblical Archaeological Review) that the temple sanctuary had previously stood a hundred metres or so to the north of the Dome of the Rock; but other specialists are adamant that the Dome of the Rock would have to go. So the historical difficulties of building the Second Temple seem to pale into insignificance alongside the present obstacles in the way of constructing a third! How the technical and political problems surrounding the third holiest site in all of Islam will be resolved, the Bible doesn't say. But the apostle Paul's words clearly imply that the third temple will be built. What's more his words agree with the message of the prophet Daniel in the Old Testament who speaks of:

> "... *the prince who is to come ... will make a firm covenant with the many for one week, but in the middle of the week he will put a stop to sacrifice and grain offering; and on the wing of abominations will come one who makes desolate, even until a complete destruction, one that is decreed, is poured out on the one who makes desolate"* (Daniel 9:24-27 NASB).

The reference is to the holy city of the Jews and to the most holy place. It simply cannot be anything other than Jerusalem and the Temple Mount area. Daniel directs our attention to *the prince who is to come* and this prince corresponds with the apostle Paul's description of the same person as the lawless one. So, two and a half thousand years ago, Daniel gave some clue as to how the third temple will come about. Daniel wrote *of "a firm covenant ... for one week"* (or literally one 'seven'). We can interpret this prophecy by laying this verse alongside others in Daniel and in Revelation: these make clear that the time period denoted by 'seven' is a reference to a seven-year period - a week of years, if you like. What Daniel is telling us is that a world leader will succeed in signing a seven-year peace deal with Israel.

As well as guaranteeing the security of Israel's borders, this treaty appears to make provision for the construction of the Third Temple. Israelites will once again offer *"sacrifice and grain offering* there". At least they will be able to do it until their 'false Messiah' turns round and rips up the deal he had signed with them. Perhaps that's when he blatantly begins to oppose the principle of law and even God himself. Like some leaders in the Middle East or Central Asia and other places today, he will start to demand idolatrous worship in the way some emperors of Rome did long ago. And he'll base himself in the Jerusalem Temple! It's presumably completed by then, having been operational for sacrifices during the preceding three and a half years. With the words of Daniel and Paul, Jesus' own words are in full agreement as they predict the future desecration of a Jerusalem temple. Jesus spoke of a time when ...

> *"... lawlessness is increased ... and then the end shall come. Therefore when you see the abomination of desolation which was spoken of through Daniel the prophet, standing in the holy place (let the reader understand), then let those who are in Judea flee to the mountains"* (Matthew 24:12-16 NASB).

Jewish Christians may have recalled these words when the Roman army carried their ensigns with the emperor's image into the temple courts in AD 70, and then went on to offer sacrifices to them. But these words are destined to have a fuller, more terrible fulfilment when a third temple is desecrated (yes, even more terrible than the detestable desecration of the Jerusalem Temple in the 2nd century BC under Antiochus Epiphanes). That's another of our golden rules for understanding Bible prophecy: there may well be partial fulfilments or secondary applications before the main fulfilment!

* **Such a view also denies:**

- the reality of distinct dispensations

TOMORROW'S HEADLINES: THE FUTURE IN BIBLE PROPHECY

- the distinction between Israel & the Church
- the unique & Jewish nature of the Great Tribulation
- and the doctrine of imminence (James 5:8)

CHAPTER EIGHT: OIL POLITICS AND OLD PROPHECIES

The world as we know it today is addicted to fossil fuels. Oil drives our western economy: it spins the turbines, heats homes and powers our vehicles. In short, it defines western civilization. Because of that it has the power to shape future events very dramatically. Many believe that recent and current events in and around the Middle East have a lot to do with securing the oil supply. It may even be that they can begin to throw some light on Bible prophecies. Saudi Arabia, Iraq and Kuwait together account for somewhere approaching 50% of the world's proven oil reserves. And as we head on through the 21st century, the world - and Europe in particular - has a dependence on Middle East oil - oil which is found under the sands of the most politically unstable region of the world. In 1990, when Saddam Hussein invaded Kuwait, he doubled the amount of oil under his control - overnight - to 25% of the world's proven reserves. Reports then hinted he might even have been planning to send his forces into Saudi Arabia too, raising the spectre of one man controlling up to half the world's oil supply.

But what if one man - whoever he might be - really could achieve a monopoly over much of the world's oil? It's no longer far-fetched to see how an oil-rich city, and its leader, could become very influential as well as fabulously wealthy. When another war against Iraq was first threatened, features in Guardian Unlimit-

TOMORROW'S HEADLINES: THE FUTURE IN BIBLE PROPHECY

ed, the New York Times and CBC News painted a graphic picture of how miserable life was in and around Babylon - 50 miles to the south of Baghdad. Miserable for ordinary Iraqis that is; life would be far from miserable in the magnificent palace overlooking the ancient site of the biblical Babylon. It was built by and for Saddam Hussein, the self-styled latter-day Nebuchadnezzar.

But the fact remains that Babylon has undergone something of a rebuilding program in recent times. Compare this with the world-wide influence and ostentatious affluence the Bible can be interpreted as predicting for an actual rebuilt Babylon in its end-time scenario. Despite the present rebuilding, it's hard to match the circumstances of a present-day Babylon with its description as influential and affluent in the Book of Revelation. Surely Babylon could never again become so influential? After all, hasn't Iraq been left crippled beyond hope of recovery? Early assessments of the damage Iraq suffered in the Gulf War of 1991 were over-estimated. That war ended with Saddam Hussein still in control of Iraq. Ironically, he remained in power longer than George Bush Senior, the driving force behind the Allied Coalition that attempted to oust him. So in some respects the Gulf War of 1991 didn't change all that much in the Middle East. Could the same thing happen again, despite initial appearances - and even with regime change? Iraq became a major military force in the region, after having been helped on its way in the mid-80s by the very western powers that have lately begun to oppose it. At that time it was cultivated as a defensive shield against Ayatollah Khomeini in order to hold Iranian revolutionary forces in check. Perhaps at that time it was anti-western religious extremists in Iran who needed to be prevented from controlling the world's oil supply?

At any rate, it demonstrates how situations get turned around in the world of international politics. With up to 50% of the earth's proven oil reserves ranged around the shores of the Persian Gulf, the potential for Iraq's rapid rise to fabulous wealth and international influence still exists. For the doubters, it need only be remembered how the discovery of oil in 1935 in Saudi Arabia transformed a group of bedouins into billionaires and changed the face of the Middle East. If oil wealth was appropriately used, the same potential still exists in Iraq. In addition, any involvement of American and European aid in postwar reconstruction could make the rebuilding programme at Babylon even more successful. In the Bible book of Revelation - a book that demands careful reading because it's rich in symbolism, we read of *"a woman sitting on a scarlet beast"* (Revelation 17:3 NASB) The Book of Revelation identifies the woman on the beast as Babylon. And the beast on which the woman sits is described as the world superpower which the prophet Daniel predicted as coming to prominence at the time of the end.

Coming back to this strange apocalyptic image of a woman astride a scarlet beast, we ask ourselves: "Can that really be predicting that control over a unified Europe will one day be wielded from the rebuilt city of Babylon (described at length in Revelation 18)?" Or is 'Babylon' just a code word for something else? Or, in the alternative view, we've been acknowledging, it would be Babylon wielding influence over Middle-eastern countries. The issue of whether Bible prophecies concerning 'Babylon' need to be understood in terms of the rebuilt ancient city has long

TOMORROW'S HEADLINES: THE FUTURE IN BIBLE PROPHECY

been an intriguing one, but there's also another explanation as to why the name Babylon crops up in Bible prophecy. Students of religious history tell us that the impact of ancient Babylon can scarcely be exaggerated. Babylon had already developed quite a religious system by the time of the Bible character of Nimrod, a great-grandson of Noah, whom we meet in Genesis chapter 10.

Ancient sources indicate that his wife founded this religious system which was a counterfeit of God's truth. The names changed wherever it was exported but its basic feature, the cult of mother and child, stayed the same. So the Phoenicians talked of Astoreth and Tammuz, and being seafarers, they carried the mother and child cult to the ends of the earth. In Egypt they became Isis and Horus; in Italy they became Venus and Cupid; while the Canaanites knew them as Asherah and Baal.

A king called Cyrus expelled the cult from Babylon in the 6th century BC, but later Julius Caesar brought it to Rome, made Rome its centre in fact, and took upon himself the title of its chief priest, the Pontifex Maximus. So already in history Babylon has ruled over Rome in a religious sense. It could be that what was true in the past will reach its full extent in the future – a counterfeit religious philosophy whose roots somehow can be traced to Babylon will hold sway over a European bloc of countries drawn from roughly the same geographical extent as the old Roman Empire. But it's not too difficult nowadays to imagine an individual controlling the oil wealth of the Middle East and using his billions to further develop the reconstruction of Babylon. An oil-rich city could use oil as a lever to exert influence over an oil-thirsty Europe. That, too, would certainly satisfy the wording found in Revelation: *"the woman whom you saw is the great city, which reigns over the kings of the earth"* (Revelation 17:18 NASB).

If we are sceptical, it's probably because we are thinking of the technology and fire-power of the west - but any dominant military power in the world would be handicapped by a dependence on oil. Even the world's strongest fighting machine grinds to a halt without oil! Any world leader emerging from a unified Europe would probably need the cooperation of a Middle Eastern ruler who had control of the world's oil reserves - unless you take the view that Europe's leader after destroying the apostate religious influence of Babylon, presides for a while over Europe from Babylon as his own new political headquarters - so in that case Europe is ruled by its own leader, but from Babylon. That also would fit the Bible picture.

We're not claiming to have a conclusive view of all the details - far from it. In relation to the Islamic theory (as opposed to the Roman theory), the more relevant aspect of tracing the religious influence of Babylon back to its roots, would be its advocacy of the moon god, 'Sin.' This crops up in our Bibles in terms of place names such as 'the wilderness of Sin,' 'Sinai,' 'Sennacherib etc. This obviously is significant in terms of the crescent moons on mosques and flags.

Whichever way you look at it, the Bible's focus on Europe probably still catches us somewhat unprepared for it. Europe has changed a great deal in the past decade. Its combined population and Gross National Product already eclipses that of the U.S. What the Bible's prophetic picture lacks at this moment is a dominant personality. A leader who will galvanize the various factions on the continent of Europe and unify them into the economic and military powerhouse of the world – but one, for a time, coming under the influence of Babylon. Probably, it's that idea that takes even more getting used to. As we've said, this influence that Babylon exerts over Europe could either be because Europe's own leader at some point begins to rule remotely from there, or because he is forced to cooperate, for a while at least, with someone else there - in Babylon - who controls the Middle East's oil reserves.

Let me reassure you that we would certainly wish to acknowledge there are different views on detailed matters of prophecy. Is it oil or Islam that's depicted as controlling either European lands or Middle-eastern lands? These scenarios are simply offered as examples which appear to satisfy the grotesque combination of woman and beast depicted in Revelation chapter 17. What we can be sure of is that there is a plan for this world. It prominently features Israel, as well as 'Babylon'. Sometime soon, perhaps, the pieces will move smoothly into place like parts of a well-oiled machine.

CHAPTER NINE: WAR IN IRAQ

Our title could have been culled from fairly recent news reports. It wasn't. It's drawn from Bible prophecies made 2,000-2,500 years ago. The Bible indicates that some future war on Iraq will be decisive. The city of Babylon is singled out for destruction. For that to happen, it must first of all exist. Which means that the current rebuilding programme there, despite whatever setbacks occur, seems destined to be a tremendous success. The area around Babylon may even benefit from post-war reconstruction efforts by western powers. Our comment on the success of this is based on the space devoted to Babylon as far as the Bible's scheme of future events goes. That, of course, begs the question as to whether this has to be understood in terms of a literal city 50 miles south of Baghdad in modern Iraq. But it's hard not to come to that conclusion, I suggest, when we weigh all the biblical evidence. Major predictions in both the Old and New Testaments converge on Babylon. But let me again make it clear that we need to allow for more than one way of seeing how these detailed prophecies will eventually be fulfilled.

Whatever else is included in this end-time Babylon, God does identify it as a city in Revelation chapter 17(v.18) - a city described more fully in the following chapter, but always in the same terms. (compare with 17:2 & 18:3,9; 17:4 & 18:16; 17:5 & 18:2; 17:6 & 18:24; 17:18 & 18:10,21; 17:17 & 19:2). God also calls it a mystery to make clear that he'd not revealed this truth about Babylon before (17:7). The mystery as now revealed to the apostle John seems to be this indication of Babylon's rise to prominence at the time of the end. However, the Bible's predictions really major on the fall of Babylon. Its sudden demise has a massive impact on world trade: *"The merchants of the earth weep and mourn over her, because no one buys their cargoes any more"*, Revelation 18:11 (NASB) says.

Prior to her downfall, Babylon is described as having become a major commercial centre, albeit one thats repeatedly said to be morally corrupt (18:3). Mention of the immorality of the Babylon of Revelation (17:2,4,5; 18:3,9) is usually thought to portray its totally false religious character - a dimension of things which historically has been very significant. Old Testament prophecies by Zechariah, Isaiah and Jeremiah all predicted that Babylon would be restored as a major power in God's future programme. Zechariah tells us how in his own words:

> *"... the angel who was speaking to me came forward and said to me, "Look up and see what this is that is appearing." I asked, "What is it?" He replied, "It is a measuring basket." And he added, "This is the iniquity of the people throughout the land." Then the cover of lead was raised, and there in the basket sat a woman! He said, "This is wickedness," and he pushed her back into the basket and pushed the lead cover down over its mouth ... "Where are they taking the basket?" I asked the angel who was speaking to me. He replied, "To the country of Babylonia to build a house for it. When it is ready, the basket will be set there in its place"* (Zechariah 5:5-11 NIV).

Again, as in Revelation, it's the symbolism of a woman that is used to represent Babylon; and again it's described as wicked, with the measuring basket possibly indicating its role as a trade centre. But, as we said, even the Old Testament prophets spent more time foretelling the fall of Babylon. Isaiah wrote:

> *"And Babylon, the beauty of kingdoms, the glory of the Chaldeans' pride, will be as when God overthrew Sodom and Gomorrah. It will never be inhabited or lived in from generation to generation; nor will the Arab pitch his tent there, nor will shepherds make their flocks lie down there. But desert creatures will lie down there, and their houses will be full of owls ... hyenas will howl in their fortified towers and jackals in their luxurious palaces. Her {fateful} time also will soon come and her days will not be prolonged. When the LORD will have compassion on Jacob, and again choose Israel, and settle them in their own land"* (Isaiah 13:19-14:1 NASB).

Isn't it interesting that Isaiah wrote of the fall of Babylon just prior to giving his prediction of Israel's restoration at the time of the end? And the prophet Jeremiah's words are like an echo of Isaiah's. He writes:

> *"As when God overthrew Sodom and Gomorrah with its neighbors," declares the LORD, "No man will live there, nor will any son of man reside in it. Behold, a people is coming from the north, and a great nation and many kings will be aroused from the remote parts of the earth... hear the plan of the LORD which He has planned against Babylon ... At the shout, "Babylon has*

TOMORROW'S HEADLINES: THE FUTURE IN BIBLE PROPHECY

> *been seized!" the earth is shaken ... "I shall dispatch foreigners to Babylon that they may ... devastate her land ... Flee from the midst of Babylon, and each of you save his life! Do not be destroyed in her punishment, for this is the LORD'S time of vengeance; He is going to render recompense to her. Babylon has been a golden cup in the hand of the LORD, intoxicating all the earth. The nations have drunk of her wine; therefore the nations are going mad. Suddenly Babylon has fallen and been broken; wail over her!"* (Jeremiah 50:40-51:8 NASB).

So much of that ties in so closely with the account of Babylon's fall in the book of Revelation (18:3,4,10,11) that it's difficult to avoid the conclusion that they all point to the same real future event. All the more so, because the fall of ancient Babylon was a gradual one. The city of Babylon rebelled in the days of the Persian empire, and it's said that Alexander the Great died there. That's why we believe the dramatic end which the Bible predicts for Babylon is still to come. Perhaps, Daniel also gave a hint of Babylon's fate - although without naming names. But when speaking of the coming world dictator (the king of the North), he said:

> *"And at the end time the king of the South will collide with him* [the king of the North] *... He will also enter the Beautiful Land, and many countries will fall; but these will be rescued out of his hand: Edom, Moab and the foremost of the sons of Ammon ... the land of Egypt will not escape... But rumors from the East and from the North will disturb him, and he will go forth with*

> *great wrath to destroy and annihilate many"* (Daniel 11:40-45 NASB).

From the south (of Israel) trouble will arise. Egypt is named as being on the receiving end. Then, probably about the same time, the northern leader (European or Islamic or both – perhaps from Turkey?) will make a forcible entry into Israel, described by Daniel here as *the beautiful land*. He'll already have torn up the peace deal he had signed which for a while had favoured Israel. And yet it seems the land of Jordan (Ammon - Amman) is to be spared from this dictator's clutches.

But then Daniel goes on to speak about rumours from the East and North. Now I'm just wondering if these rumours which disturb the world leader might have anything to do with Babylon - Babylon is certainly east and north of the last-mentioned area. Could these rumours be the trigger for him to go and finally destroy it and so be rid of its control over him? At that point it seems the world's heading for Armageddon. Nearly everyone's heard of Armageddon! Its Bible mention in the book of Revelation comes just before the section which tells us about Babylon's destruction. So there could be a connection. The Bible doesn't actually speak of a single last battle being fought at Armageddon, but the evidence points to it being a rallying point for a series of battles in the time of the end. Let's remind ourselves of what the Bible does say:

> *"And the sixth angel poured out his bowl upon the great river, the Euphrates; and its water was dried up, that the way might be prepared for the kings from the east. And I saw coming out of the mouth of the dragon and*

out of the mouth of the beast and out of the mouth of the false prophet, three unclean spirits like frogs; for they are spirits of demons, performing signs, which go out to the kings of the whole world, to gather them together for the war of the great day of God, the Almighty ... And they gathered them together to the place which in Hebrew is called Har-Magedon. And the seventh angel poured out his bowl upon the air; and a loud voice came out of the temple from the throne, saying, "It is done."... And the great city was split into three parts, and the cities of the nations fell. And Babylon the great was remembered before God, to give her the cup of the wine of His fierce wrath" (Revelation 16:12-19 NASB).

Armageddon, it seems, is a gathering point for this international task force from the east. In one view, they gather to prepare an attack against the Antichrist's own adopted power-base in Babylon. But perhaps there's no compelling evidence to suggest they gather as enemies. They could, in fact, be gathering as allies of the northern leader. In this alternative view, after he's destroyed Egypt and invaded Israel, perhaps these eastern allies join forces with him against an oil-rich Babylon. Whichever way, the fall of Babylon is mentioned straight after we read of the gathering of this task force from the east. Of course, there's never any guarantee in Bible prophecies that events mentioned together actually follow closely in time sequence. But the main point is that this destruction of Babylon is effectively God's judgement against it.

CHAPTER TEN: HOLOCAUST & OPERATION JERUSALEM

Writing of the end of the Antichrist's reign of terror, Daniel says: *"And he will pitch the tents of his royal pavilion between the seas and the beautiful Holy Mountain; yet he will come to his end, and no one will help him"* (Daniel 11:45 NASB). Between the Mediterranean and Dead seas lies the 'beautiful holy mountain' of Jerusalem. The Antichrist and his allies go there not knowing that their end is near. It's interesting to remember that this world leader - the lawless one as the apostle Paul describes him - first appeared on the scene as a man of peace. He was hailed as the answer to Europe's prayers. In a masterstroke beyond the imagination of any of today's political pundits, he resolved the long-standing issue of Middle Eastern conflict - much to the relief and admiration of the international community.

But within three and a half years he showed his true colours, meriting the Bible's characterization of him as 'the beast'. His thirst for power seems insatiable. He seems to hold the world spellbound. When he recovers from a fatal wound, the world stands in awe of him. The apostle John wrote in Revelation: *"Who is like the beast, and who is able to wage war with him?"* ... *the earth and those who dwell in it ... worship the ... beast, whose fatal wound was healed"* (Revelation 13:4,12 NASB).

This world is not yet done with emperors who pursue world domination and demand divine honours. After the destruction

TOMORROW'S HEADLINES: THE FUTURE IN BIBLE PROPHECY

of Babylon, this latter-day dictator - in his own on-going attempt to eradicate any remaining pockets of resistance - finally turns his attention on Jerusalem. His relationship with Israel and Jerusalem is a complex one. Seven years earlier he had signed the famous peace deal that had paved the way for the building of the third Jewish temple there. But in three and a half years he was back - no longer as a benefactor - but as a desecrator. It was around that time that many Jews fled the land of Israel (possibly for Jordan) while others preferred terrible persecution rather than acknowledge this false Messiah. The roots of anti-Semitism run deep, and with a most definite Satanic twist. Satan's antagonism against them is unmasked by the apostle John.

We are told it's due to the fact that the Jews were God's chosen vehicle in bringing the Son of God into human experience. The planned sacrificial death of Jesus Christ on a Roman cross, sealed Satan's own fate, and in a vain fury at his own inability to frustrate God's purpose through Jesus Christ, Satan's hostility turned against the Jews instead. The apostle John saw it all under the imagery of Satan as the dragon and Israel as the woman:

> *"And when the dragon saw that he was thrown down to the earth, he persecuted the woman who gave birth to the male child.* [that's Jesus] *And the two wings of the great eagle were given to the woman, in order that she might fly into the wilderness to her place, where she was nourished for a time and times and half a time, from the presence of the serpent ... And the dragon was enraged with the woman, and went off to make war with the rest of her offspring, who keep the commandments*

of God and hold to the testimony of Jesus" (Revelation 12:13-17 NASB).

So, ultimately, there's something deeply Satanic about anti-Semitism: the persecution of Jews. Israel's Yad Vashem holocaust museum is currently a moving reminder of the holocaust when six million Jews were wiped out during the war against Nazism. Sadly, Europe has not yet learned its lesson. We have John's words: *"If anyone is destined for captivity, to captivity he goes; if anyone kills with the sword, with the sword he must be killed"* (Revelation 13:10 NASB).

During the second half of the reign of the world dictator known biblically as the beast, there will be a time of unprecedented tribulation for the nation of Israel especially, but affecting all who refuse to own allegiance to the man then at the helm of Europe. A fearful final holocaust will take its terrible toll in the death camps of the beast. This will be the time of 'Jacob's distress' (Jeremiah 30:7, preceding the future application to Israel of the New Covenant in chapter 31). We must be sure to distinguish 'the elect of those days' (Matthew 24:22) from the elect of the present Church Age. The Church does not pass through the Tribulation (1 Thessalonians 5:9), but in each age or dispensation of God's dealings with men and women, his sovereign arrangements include the provision of salvation.

As the pocket of Israeli resistance intensifies, the prophet Daniel predicts this leader will again visit the land of Israel, but the visit will take the form of forcible entry (Daniel 11:41). Daniel says: *"he will stretch out his hand against other countries ... he will gain control"* (11:42,43). At this point he seems to be in the business

TOMORROW'S HEADLINES: THE FUTURE IN BIBLE PROPHECY

of settling scores or is engaged in mopping up operations. Energized by a Satanic hatred of Jews, his attention finally shifts to that other ancient city - Jerusalem. This will be his last mission. Jerusalem becomes ground zero - as with all his allies - he moves to eliminate the last Jewish resistance there. We'll let the prophet Joel take up the story, for the script is already written:

> *"Proclaim this among the nations: prepare a war; rouse the mighty men! Let all the soldiers draw near, let them come up! Beat your plowshares into swords, and your pruning hooks into spears; let the weak say, "I am a mighty man." Hasten and come, all you surrounding nations, and gather yourselves there. Bring down, O LORD, [Your] mighty ones. Let the nations be aroused and come up to the valley of Jehoshaphat, for there I will sit to judge all the surrounding nations. Put in the sickle, for the harvest is ripe. Come, tread, for the wine press is full; the vats overflow, for their wickedness is great. Multitudes, multitudes in the valley of decision! For the day of the LORD is near in the valley of decision"* (Joel 3:9-14 NASB).

Multitudes in the valley of decision or judgement - but the outcome has already been decided. The outcome of this last attack on Jerusalem before Christ returns to earth is not in any doubt. This valley of decision may well turn out to be the one that runs to the east of Jerusalem city, dividing it from the Mount of Olives. Certainly, the prophet Zechariah makes mention of a very special event at the Mount of Olives - in what must be another description of this same battle:

> *"For I will gather all the nations against Jerusalem to battle, and the city will be captured, the houses plundered, the women ravished, and half of the city exiled, but the rest of the people will not be cut off from the city. Then the LORD will go forth and fight against those nations, as when He fights on a day of battle. And in that day His feet will stand on the Mount of Olives, which is in front of Jerusalem on the east; and the Mount of Olives will be split in its middle from east to west by a very large valley, so that half of the mountain will move toward the north and the other half toward the south"* (Zechariah 14:2-4 NASB).

The reason this battle is decisive is that it is brought to an end by the return of the Lord Jesus Christ to liberate Jerusalem. This is the second stage of Christ's Second Advent. In this book, we have already anticipated this event when we quoted Paul as he in turn quoted Isaiah's forecast that a Deliverer would*"… come to Zion, and to those who turn from transgression in Jacob," declares the LORD"* (Isaiah 59:20 NASB). This is God's mighty intervention on behalf of his ancient people. The touch down of the Lord's feet on the Mount of Olives settles this climactic showdown with the Antichrist. The Lord descends on the spot from which two thousand years ago he ascended after his resurrection. The apostle John in his last book of the Revelation draws aside the veil and sees the Lord returning at this same point in time at the head of the armies of heaven, and with the result that:

> *"… the beast* [the Antichrist at the helm of Europe] *was seized, and with him the false prophet who per-*

formed the signs in his presence, by which he deceived those who had received the mark of the beast and those who worshiped his image; these two were thrown alive into the lake of fire which burns with brimstone" (Revelation 19:20 NASB).

Since these things are shortly about to happen, we must *"testify solemnly to the gospel of the grace of God"* (Acts 20:24). A similar fate awaits all who reject the salvation that is only to be found in God's Son, Jesus Christ.

CHAPTER ELEVEN: THE RISE OF ISLAM

So far we appear not to have said too much about the future influence of the Arab or Muslim world - although we ought to clarify that not all Arabs are Muslims. And although we have looked at the Middle East, it's also worth remembering that a middle eastern country like Iran has a mainly Persian - not Arabic - population. We must not forget there are those differences between the labels middle eastern, Arabic and Muslim.

In our review of Bible prophecies up to this point, as far as the Middle East is concerned, we have touched on Egypt and Jordan while majoring on Israel and Iraq. But what about the great swathe of Islamic countries from the central Asian republic of Kazakhstan right round to the Western Sahara of northern Africa? To the south and west, as well as to the east and north of Israel, there's an impressive, wide arc of predominantly Islamic countries. Do the Bible prophecies have anything to say about this? From Israel's point of view it must seem like an intimidating swathe of countries which sweeps down from Kazakhstan through Iran, Iraq, Saudi Arabia and on to Algeria and her Saharan neighbours. Just how real is any threat to Israel? Does the Bible indicate hostility against Israel coming from this quarter? The key section is found in Ezekiel's prophecy:

> *"And the word of the LORD came to me saying, Son of man, set your face toward Gog of the land of Magog, the prince of Rosh, Meshech, and Tubal, and prophesy*

against him, and say, 'Thus says the Lord GOD, "Behold, I am against you, O Gog, prince of Rosh, Meshech, and Tubal. And I will turn you about ..."

These names probably don't mean much - if anything - to us. The key question is: which parts of the world did they refer to at the time when the prophecy was written? For at least 900 years before that time (see Genesis 10), these place names were attached to the areas we know today as Turkey, and the countries between the Black and Caspian Seas like Armenia, Azerbaijan, Georgia, and the southern tip of Russia along with north western Iran. It is a fascinating focus on Turkey. Turkey looks west and east in today's world. It is recognized as a key player in the region. It - or especially its government - has in the recent past maintained close ties with the west, but on account of its Islamic population, it has also begun to look eastwards for support. It has been active (since 1989) in promoting the Black Sea Economic Cooperation Zone. A sort of 'common market' that includes Armenia, Azerbaijan, Georgia and Russia alongside Turkey.

In addition, Turkey has obvious cultural and religious ties with Central Asian countries (former Soviet Republics) like Kazakhstan and Turkmenistan. Both Turkey and Iran have been trying to woo these countries. What is interesting is that today we can see some kind of alliance emerging between countries which the Bible predicts will ultimately be in alliance with each other. More than that, they will be the leaders of an invasion against Israel, as prophesied by Ezekiel. For he spoke of an attack on Israel carried out by people who would be living in the general area of Turkey and the land between the Black and Caspian Seas. But

Ezekiel (38:5-8) goes on to mention other nations who will join with those countries:

> *"Persia, Ethiopia, and Put with them, all of them with shield and helmet; Gomer with all its troops; Beth-togarmah from the remote parts of the north with all its troops - many peoples with you. Be prepared, and prepare yourself, you and all your companies that are assembled about you, and be a guard for them."*

Heading this second list is Persia, which is modern-day Iran. Iranians today speak the Persian (or Farsi) language. Next in line to be mentioned by Ezekiel is 'Cush'. Earlier in his prophecy (29:10), Ezekiel has shown that by Cush he's referring to an area south of Egypt in the region known to us as Sudan and Ethiopia. Then there is 'Put' which is generally accepted as being Libya, to the west of Egypt. Students of Bible prophecy have been scratching their heads for a long time over this unlikely assortment of countries seemingly indicated by Ezekiel long ago. What would Turkey and some former republics of the Soviet Union have in common with Iran, Sudan and Libya? Why should they conspire together to launch an attack on Israel? The best answer now emerging may seem to be Islam, and the rise of Islamic fundamentalism.

A report surfaced in an Arab language magazine some time back which claimed that Iran used the confusion following the collapse of the Soviet Union to purchase nuclear weapons from Kazakhstan. Iranian influence is also growing in Sudan. Apparently, it sent its Revolutionary Guards to train the Sudanese army as well to supply military equipment. And, of course,

Libya's opposition to Israel is well known. Turkey, Iran, the Muslim republics, Sudan and Libya. Countries with little in common - except their Islamic faith - and the fact that Ezekiel implicates them in an attack on Israel. For thousands of years this alliance seemed improbable, but it seems as if at last a grouping - with Turkey and Iran as prime movers - may indeed be starting to show signs of coming together. The big question, of course, is when will any attack take place? Coming back to Ezekiel's prophecy again, we find:

> *"After many days you will be summoned; in the latter years you will come into the land that is restored from the sword, {whose inhabitants} have been gathered from many nations to the mountains of Israel which had been a continual waste; but its people were brought out from the nations, and they are living securely, all of them"* (Ezekiel 38:1-8 NASB).

It is something of a puzzle to know quite when this prediction of Ezekiel applies. It is said to be at a time when Israel feels secure. *'The land ... restored from the sword ... [will be] living securely.'* Weighing all of Ezekiel's clues (37:24-26; 38:8,23; 39:9, 21-23), it may be better to set this among the Lord's judgements of the nations after the time when he himself has come as a deliverer to Zion. It is then that LORD *"makes himself known in the sight of many nations".* A time when Israel may be described as *"the land restored from the sword."* Besides that, we have already seen a pattern to Ezekiel's writing - one which seems to set out a series of events in relative time sequence. These prophecies about this coalition of forces coming against Israel are sandwiched between Ezekiel's vision of Israel's revival - pictured in the valley of dry bones (ch.37) - and his vision of what we take to be the future Millennial Temple (ch.40).

In the chapter before we read of this attack, we are told that God's Spirit will take up Israel and they will be fully gathered into their land and united as one undivided nation (Ezekiel 37:14,21,22). God will be in their midst and the nations will know it (Ezekiel 37:23,27,28). Do these things not require the return of Jesus Christ to this earth to bring them about? And come he will - to reign for a thousand years. The apostle John in his vision of the future in Rev 20:1-15 saw an angel who:

> *"... laid hold of ... Satan, and bound him for a thousand years ... And I [John] saw thrones, and they sat upon them, and judgment was given to them. And I saw the souls of those who had been beheaded because of the testimony of Jesus and because of the word of God, and those who had not worshiped the beast or his image, and had not received the mark upon their forehead and upon their hand; and they came to life and reigned with Christ for a thousand years. The rest of the dead did not come to life until the thousand years were completed. This is the first resurrection ... when the thousand years are completed, Satan will be released from his prison, and will come out to deceive the nations which are in the four corners of the earth, Gog and Magog, to gather them together for the war; the number of them is like the sand of the seashore. And they came up on the broad plain of the earth and surrounded the camp of the saints and the beloved city, and fire came down from heaven*

and devoured them. And the devil who deceived them was thrown into the lake of fire ..."

Firstly, let's again notice the fact that there will be those who will be saved during the great tribulation, having refused to receive the Antichrist's mark and worship his image. They are part of this first (in association with the Millennium) resurrection. Also, from the Lord's parable of the separation of the sheep from the goats (Matthew 25:32-34), we note that as well as those who have been raised and judged worthy of entrance into Christ's Millennial kingdom, there will be those who are alive on earth when the Lord returns to the earth - people in ordinary bodies - who will be admitted into the kingdom too. From among the ranks of this latter category (and their descendants) will come this final revolt by Gog and Magog. We underline this to clarify that once any are raised in their new bodies and enter into blessedness, there is no prospect of them ever again succumbing to sin.

It is most interesting, that at the close of this thousand years of peace, nations again described as 'Gog and Magog' are said to gather to besiege Jerusalem. If this was the same attack that Ezekiel described, it would hardly seem that the current trends we noted earlier could have any bearing on it. But if the thousand years of peace end with an attack from this region, is it not even more probable that it begins with one as well? This is what we are suggesting, for the Millennium follows on from the most turbulent of times when God's judgements on the nations are still being carried out. In which case, the modern alliances between countries with a common Islamic heritage could well be a factor. However, if the timing of the attack is in doubt, the outcome is not in any doubt. For Ezekiel says of Israel's attackers: *"You shall fall on the mountains of Israel, you and all your troops, and the peoples who are with you; I shall give you as food to every kind of predatory bird and beast of the field"* (Ezekiel 39:4 NASB).

CHAPTER TWELVE: MAJOR TRENDS

Let us restate what we can be sure of about the time of the end - and beyond: We can know, on the authority of God's Word, the Bible, that:

1. Christ will return to the air for His Church; and that

2. The Antichrist will afterward rise to power; and so

3. Earth will have unprecedented trouble; and then

4. Christ will return to the earth itself; and

5. He will rule for 1,000 years; then

6. Christ will judge unbelievers; when finally

7. A new world will be created.

It remains for us to cover those last points. Bible-believing Christians know that history is headed somewhere. One day Jesus Christ will judge the nations at the beginning of His thousand year reign on this earth. The same person whom the first century Jewish leaders judged to be an impostor, and had crucified on a cross, will return to this earth in glory and rule the nations with a rod of iron (Revelation 12:5). As the Bible prophet, Isaiah, predicted: a king shall reign in righteousness (Isaiah 32:1) and the earth will enjoy peace and all of nature will be in harmony:

> *"The cow and the bear shall graze; their young ones shall lie down together; and the lion shall eat straw like the ox. The nursing child shall play by the cobra's hole, and the weaned child shall put his hand in the viper's den. They shall not hurt nor destroy in all My holy mountain, for the earth shall be full of the knowledge of the LORD as the waters cover the sea"* (Isaiah 11:7-9).

Then from the same prophet, Isaiah, but from chapter 65 we read:

> *"They shall build houses and inhabit them; they shall plant vineyards and eat their fruit. They shall not build and another inhabit; they shall not plant and another eat; for as the days of a tree, so shall be the days of My people, and My elect shall long enjoy the work of their hands ... The wolf and the lamb shall feed together, the lion shall eat straw like the ox, and dust shall be the serpent's food. They shall not hurt nor destroy in all My holy mountain," says the LORD."*

And again from the Bible book of the prophet Isaiah, this time chapter 35:

> *"The wilderness and the wasteland shall be glad for them, and the desert shall rejoice and blossom as the rose; It shall blossom abundantly and rejoice, even with joy and singing. Then the lame shall leap like a deer, and the tongue of the dumb sing. For waters shall burst forth in the wilderness, and streams in the desert. The parched ground shall become a pool, and the thirsty land springs*

of water; in the habitation of jackals, where each lay, there shall be grass with reeds and rushes."

This earth will be a wonderful place when the Lord Jesus Christ rules! This world has had a very chequered history to say the least, but the best is yet to come! - that is if you are a believer. After that golden rule of a thousand years on this earth, and after Satan's last stand has ended with the Devil being assigned for ever to the lake of fire which was prepared specially for him, God is going to complete his judgements on all who have ever lived on the earth throughout history. This is often called the great white throne judgement because of what we read in verse 11 of Revelation chapter 20: *"Then I saw a great white throne and Him who sat upon it ... And I saw the dead, the great and the small, standing before the throne, and ... the dead were judged ... And if anyone's name was not found written in the book of life, he was thrown into the lake of fire".*

Notice that 'if'. Many believe that not all will be condemned at that judgement; but that the so-called 'infant dead' and 'heathen dead' (those who died throughout history without attaining to an age of understanding or without ever having been sufficiently spiritually enlightened so as to be accountable) will pass from there into eternal blessedness. That brings a special poignancy to the Lord's words about rejoicing if our names are written in heaven. This is the case with everyone who receives the Lord Jesus into their heart by faith as the only one in whom forgiveness with God is to be found. If you're still not sure, listen to these words from Acts 17: *"God ... now commands all men everywhere to repent, because He has appointed a day on which He will judge the world in righteousness by the Man whom He has ordained. He has given assurance of this to all by raising Him from the dead."* After this it will be paradise regained for those who go into eternal blessing, as we read in Revelation 21:

> *"Now I saw a new heaven and a new earth, for the first heaven and the first earth had passed away. Also there was no more sea ... And God will wipe away every tear from their eyes; there shall be no more death, nor sorrow, nor crying. There shall be no more pain, for the former things have passed away." Then He who sat on the throne said, "Behold, I make all things new."*

We can be ready now to face the future. God can make us ready by making us new right now, even as His Word says: *"Therefore, if anyone is in Christ, he is a new creation"* (2 Corinthians 5:17). Throughout this book we have hinted at ways in which current events in the world appear to be approximating to what the Bible predicts will be the case as we approach the time of the end. Let us just summarize a few trends we can deduce from what the Bible says, things like:

1. Globalization through communications technology - in Revelation (13:12,17), we read of the future world superpower and its leader having control over buying and selling. 'The earth', it is said, will pay homage to him. Previously, that might have seemed far-fetched, but today we are used to satellite telecommunications and the global medium of the internet.
2. A cashless society with information processed through microchips implanted into our skin is no longer in the realms of science fiction.

TOMORROW'S HEADLINES: THE FUTURE IN BIBLE PROPHECY

3. Then there is the present focus on the Middle East - the fact that it has come to dominate international politics as the Bible clearly implied it would (Revelation 14; 16; Romans 9-11).
4. Another indication in Bible prophecy points to a trend towards human unification. Today we see emerging political power blocks;
5. the grouping together and rise of Islamic nations; the talk (or fear) of federalization in Europe; not to mention religious aggregation, monetary unions, and a global economy complete with interlinked markets (Revelation 17:11-13).
6. Through the prophecy of Daniel it is predicted that *knowledge will increase* (Daniel 12:4). The amazing acceleration of knowledge is something we almost take for granted in the modern world. There is the staggering pace of development in the world's so-called Silicon valleys, as well as in such fields as genetic engineering, screening, cloning, and DNA tracking - some of which brings with it an attack on the sanctity of human life (Revelation 13:15).
7. Then there is society's perception of some kind of impending disaster (Luke 21:26) - its dread of killer diseases, maybe as rogue viruses go global. We have also had examples of how the rise of lawlessness generally and acts of mass terrorism specifically have the capability to quickly de-stabilize large areas of the world.
8. Add to that the availability of weapons of mass destruction, and Revelation's large-scale death tolls

seem to make more sense. When we review global trends like those we've just mentioned, it is hard not to draw the conclusion that the time of the end, as predicted in Bible prophecy, is near.

Earlier in this book, we read in the book of Daniel about how the captive Daniel was given an insight into how the captivity the Jews were then experiencing had been predicted earlier by the prophet Jeremiah. What was more, Jeremiah had said that the period of captivity would last for 70 years, and then God's future programme for Israel would begin to be fulfilled. Now the point was - and this explains Daniel's urgent prayer - that the time for the beginning of this fulfilment had almost arrived! God gave Daniel insight shortly before the events themselves came to pass.

I now want to leave a final thought with you. I believe the 'time of the end' is not far off. We do need to allow scope for different detailed understandings of how Bible prophecy is shaping up for fulfilment, but we can be sure of the overall framework. And I wonder if, as with Daniel, we have been led by God to receive this futurist insight - because, like Daniel, we are now living close to the time when these things are to come upon us?

Did you love *Tomorrow's Headlines: The Future in Bible Prophecy*? Then you should read *Daniel Decoded: Deciphering Bible Prophecy* by Brian Johnston!

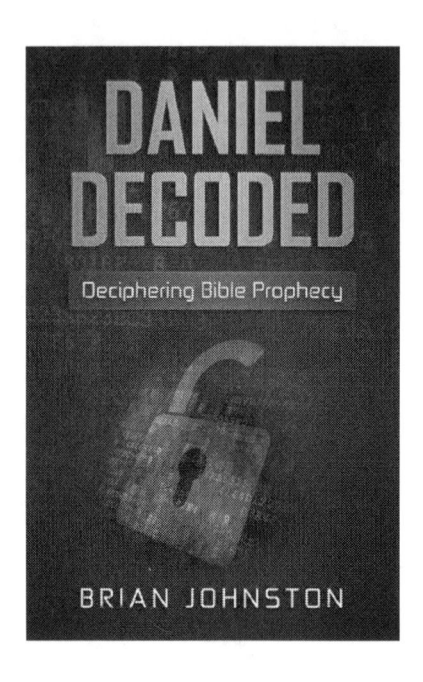

The Old Testament book of Daniel is perhaps the most half-read in all the Bible! The first half is full of well-loved Sunday School stories and the second half contains complex prophecies about the end times. Brian Johnston explores both halves in this engaging study, which will inspire and inform in equal measure!

CHAPTER ONE: MIGRANTS, AN ALIEN CULTURE AND A HAM SANDWICH
CHAPTER TWO: GOD'S MAN COMES THROUGH
CHAPTER THREE: THE WORLD'S HOTTEST FIRE
CHAPTER FOUR: BECOMING BESTIAL

CHAPTER FIVE: LET THE CRITICS EAT THEIR WORDS
CHAPTER SIX: FACED WITH INJUSTICE
CHAPTER SEVEN: THE RISE AND FALL OF WORLD EMPIRES
CHAPTER EIGHT: THE BRILLIANT MADMAN WHO HATED ISRAEL
CHAPTER NINE: DANIEL'S SEVENTY 'SEVENS'
CHAPTER TEN: SPIRITUAL WARFARE
CHAPTER ELEVEN: THE BIBLE'S MOST DETAILED PROPHETIC CHAPTER
CHAPTER TWELVE: THE END

Also by Brian Johnston

Healthy Churches - God's Bible Blueprint For Growth
Hope for Humanity: God's Fix for a Broken World
First Corinthians: Nothing But Christ Crucified
Bible Answers to Listeners' Questions
Living in God's House: His Design in Action
Christianity 101: Seven Bible Basics
Nights of Old: Bible Stories of God at Work
Daniel Decoded: Deciphering Bible Prophecy
A Test of Commitment: 15 Challenges to Stimulate Your Devotion to Christ
John's Epistles - Certainty in the Face of Change
If Atheism Is True...
Brian Johnston Box Set 1
8 Amazing Privileges of God's People: A Bible Study of Romans 9:4-5
Learning from Bible Grandparents
Increasing Your Christian Footprint
Christ-centred Faith
Mindfulness That Jesus Endorses
Amazing Grace! Paul's Gospel Message to the Galatians
Abraham: Friend of God
Tomorrow's Headlines: The Future in Bible Prophecy
Unlocking Hebrews

Learning How To Pray - From the Lord's Prayer

About the Author

Born and educated in Scotland, Brian worked as a government scientist until God called him into full-time Christian ministry on behalf of the Churches of God (www.churchesofgod.info). His voice has been heard on Search For Truth radio broadcasts for over 30 years during which time he has been an itinerant Bible teacher throughout the UK and Canada. His evangelical and missionary work outside the UK is primarily in Belgium and The Philippines. He is married to Rosemary, with a son and daughter.

About the Publisher

Hayes Press (www.hayespress.org) is a registered charity in the United Kingdom, whose primary mission is to disseminate the Word of God, mainly through literature. It is one of the largest distributors of gospel tracts and leaflets in the United Kingdom, with over 100 titles and hundreds of thousands despatched annually.

Hayes Press also publishes Plus Eagles Wings, a fun and educational Bible magazine for children, and Golden Bells, a popular daily Bible reading calendar in wall or desk formats.

Also available are over 100 Bibles in many different versions, shapes and sizes, Christmas cards, Christian jewellery, Eikos Bible Art, Bible text posters and much more!

Manufactured by Amazon.ca
Bolton, ON